ULTIMATE SPORTS

DON'T LOOK DOWN!

EXTREME AIR SPORTS

CHERITON
CHILDREN'S BOOKS

Published in 2024 by **Cheriton Children's Books**
1 Bank Drive West, Shrewsbury, Shropshire, SY3 9DJ, UK

© 2024 Cheriton Children's Books

First Edition

Author: Sarah Eason
Designer: Paul Myerscough
Editor: Jennifer Sanderson
Proofreader: Katie Dicker

Printed in China

Please visit our website,
www.cheritonchildrensbooks.com
to see more of our high-quality books.

CONTENTS

DON'T LOOK DOWN!

When you look up into the skies, you see a wide-open world that seems to stretch out forever—and a paradise playground for people who love **extreme sports**. These fans of extreme adventure head for the heights, then **freefall** or glide back down. They **scale** soaring skyscrapers and towers, then leap over the edge for the ultimate cityscape **adrenaline** rush. And they **highline, zip wire, canyon swing**, and more through Earth's most dramatic **land formations**. For Earth's **elite athletes**, the sky is the ultimate training zone.

READY TO EXPLORE THE EXTREME?...

THE EXTREME DREAM

For decades, people have loved air sports—from **gliding** and **skydiving** to **bungee jumping** and canyon swinging. But today, technology has taken our love of air sports to a whole new level. We have specialized wings that help us perform awesome **aerial acrobatics**. We have equipment that allows us to skim Earth's slopes at incredible speeds. And sport science has helped us hone our bodies to **endure** some of the most **grueling** activities in the air. We are soaring, spiraling, freefalling, and doing more than was once dreamed possible. We are taking air sports to the max.

...THEN, REACH FOR THE SKY AND DON'T LOOK DOWN!

CHAPTER 1

SKY-HIGH JUMPS

Some air sports were made for adrenaline highs, and skydiving is no exception. It is one of the ultimate adventure sports, in which skydivers jump from an aircraft and then freefall through the sky. It comes as no surprise that skydiving is considered one of the most **exhilarating** extreme sports.

JUMP AND FALL!

Skydiving involves different stages, and each one must be carefully carried out for a safe dive. First, skydivers board an aircraft, and fly to the height from where they will jump. At the jump height, the skydiver leaps out of the plane and freefalls. During a freefall, the diver **plummets** through the air at speeds of up to 120 miles per hour (193 kph).

"LIFE BEGINS AT THE END OF YOUR COMFORT ZONE."

It takes a lot of courage to jump from a plane into the air many miles above the ground!

A freefall can last for around 60 seconds.

EXTREME HISTORY

The history of skydiving may date back to ancient China, when people made parachutes from cloth and bamboo frames to slow their fall when jumping from a height or to perform acrobatic moves.

The first recorded parachute jump was made in 1797 when a Frenchman, named André-Jacques Garnerin jumped from a hot air balloon using a parachute made of silk.

SLOW THE DROP

At the correct height, the skydiver puts their parachute into action. The parachute is packed within a container attached to the skydiver's harness. When the parachute is released, it quickly opens and slows down the drop. That allows for a controlled **descent** to the ground.

LOOK AND LAND!

Once they have slowed their descent, the skydiver steers and controls the parachute using specially designed handles or toggles. Now that they are not hurtling toward the ground at breathtaking speed, the diver can enjoy the view! Finally, they touch down on the ground and land.

Parachute formation flying is an extreme team sport in which a group of skydivers performs different formations and **maneuvers** while in freefall.

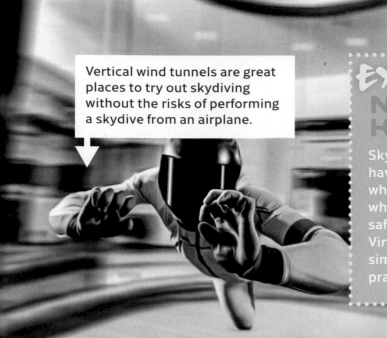

Vertical wind tunnels are great places to try out skydiving without the risks of performing a skydive from an airplane.

Skydiving training centers often have vertical wind tunnels in which people can experience what it is like to freefall in a safe and secure environment. Virtual reality (VR) parachute simulators can also be used for practicing using a parachute.

Tandem flying with an instructor is a great way for beginners to experience skydiving.

TRAINED TO DIVE

Skydiving is a specialized sport that requires special equipment—and a lot of training. Skydiving often takes place at centers where the dives are carefully controlled. Some centers offer tandem jumps, during which beginners are harnessed to an experienced instructor for their first few jumps. This allows **newbie** skydivers to experience a thrilling, but safe, dive.

AIR ACROBATS

Freeflying is the most acrobatic style of skydiving, with skydivers performing amazing moves in the air as they fall through the sky. Divers plummet head-down or feet-first, doing flips, twists, and spins as they fall. It is amazing to watch but takes hours of training to perform safely.

Skilled freefliers make air acrobatics seem easy but freeflying is one of the toughest sports to learn.

EXTREME STARS

SPACE DIVER

Felix Baumgartner is famous for completing an incredible freefall parachute jump in 2012 from a height of 127,852 feet (38,969 m). In the process, the Austrian skydiver broke eight world records—and smashed through the **sound barrier**!

EXTREME PARACHUTER

Felix began skydiving at the age of 16. He loved the experience and wanted to try out even more challenging parachuting. As his love of the sport developed, he sought out the extreme sports sponsor Red Bull to help him carry out the ultimate challenge—the highest-ever freefall parachute jump.

UP TO SPACE

On 14 October 2012, a giant balloon as tall as the Statue of Liberty was inflated, or filled, with helium gas for the jump, and in a capsule below it, Felix was carried high into the sky. It took two hours to lift him to the jump point in the **stratosphere**. Then, Felix stood on the edge of the capsule and with the words, "I'm going home now," he leaped, and fell toward Earth.

BREAKING THE SOUND BARRIER

The jump took just over 9 minutes, and Felix reached speeds of 843 miles per hour (1,357 kph), becoming the first person to ever break the sound barrier in freefall. Amongst his records, he'd also performed the highest freefall parachute jump. His spectacular stunt inspired Alan Eustace, who jumped even higher in 2014 from a height of 135,898 feet (41,422 m).

FLYING FREE

Like skydivers, wingsuit fliers head for the heights, and then jump. But they jump wearing a wingsuit as well as using a parachute. The wingsuit allows them to fly through the air with astonishing—if pretty scary—birdlike freedom.

BIRD OR HUMAN?!

Wingsuits, or birdman suits as they are sometimes called, are specially designed jumpsuits that allow people to glide through the air. The fabric wings are usually made of lightweight and **flexible** material, such as nylon or spandex. That allows for easy movement and minimal **drag**.

EXTREME HISTORY

Wingsuit flying first began in the 1930s, when a French parachutist named Léo Valentin designed and tested an early wingsuit called the "Birdman" suit. Decades later, the sport had gained fame and popularity, largely thanks to wingsuit pilots Loïc Jean-Albert and Yves Rossy, who performed some amazing flights.

Wingsuit flying is an amazing way to experience a mountain landscape—for those brave enough to try it!

"SPREAD YOUR WINGS AND LET THE WIND CARRY YOU."

A wingsuit flier uses a **spread-eagle position** during flight.

GLIDING HIGH

The wings of a wingsuit stretch between the arms and legs, which increases the flier's **surface area**. That creates lift and allows them to glide through the air for longer. The flier also reaches out their arms and legs, which further increases the wingsuit surface area.

FLIGHT CONTROL

As the wingsuit flier moves through the air, the shape of the wings creates lift. This lift acts against the force of **gravity**, allowing the flier to move horizontally and keep in the air for longer. Wingsuit fliers can even control the direction in which they move, by shifting their weight or changing the angle of their arms, legs, or **trunk**.

PARACHUTE PROTECTION

Wingsuit flying may be an adrenaline-fueled sport but all fliers have a safety backup—a parachute. When they are ready to stop their flight, they use the parachute to slow their descent and safely land.

TAKING OFF AND TAKING OVER

By the early 2000s, wingsuit flying was really taking off. Jeb Corliss, an American **BASE jumper** and wingsuit flier, took on incredible flights and stunts. The videos of his flights made wingsuit flying a worldwide sensation, and soon many other extreme sports lovers were taking up this daredevil form of flying.

THE WORLD'S BEST WINGSUIT FLIGHTS

There are some incredible locations around the world for wingsuit flying, where the awe-inspiring landscapes and challenging **flight paths** combine for the ultimate thrill of flying free. These are the top picks.

Moab

Where: Utah, United States

The draw: famous for its red rock formations and desert landscape, Moab has cliffs, canyons, and **gorges** that create stunning flight paths

Chamonix

Where: France

The draw: accessible jump-off points provide long and spectacular flights over deep ravines, glaciers, and lush, wooded valleys

Lauterbrunnen Valley

Where: Switzerland

The draw: stunning views of snow-capped peaks, lush green valleys, and beautiful waterfalls

Kjerag

Where: Norway

The draw: steep cliffs, which include the famous Kjeragbolten (a large boulder wedged between two cliffs), and stunning views of the Norwegian **fjords** below

Zhangjiajie National Forest Park

Where: Zhangjiajie, China

The draw: towering sandstone pillars, jagged peaks, and deep valleys wrapped in mist make for an out-of-this-world flight

Walenstadt

Where: Switzerland

The draw: exciting flight routes with stunning views of Lake Walen and the Swiss Alps

Dubai

Where: United Arab Emirates

The draw: with perfect weather conditions all year round and breathtaking views of the Palm Islands as you fall, this wingsuit flight starts from a plane, 13,000 ft (3,962 m) high

CLIMB AND JUMP!

BASE jumping is another adrenaline-high air sport loved by extreme sportspeople around the world. Like skydiving, it involves jumping from a high point into the air with a parachute. However, unlike skydivers, BASE jumpers leap from fixed objects rather than out of an airplane.

COVERING ALL BASES

BASE stands for Building, Antenna, Span, and Earth, which are the four main types of object used for jumps. Buildings can include tall buildings, such as skyscrapers and towers, or bridges. Antennae are radio or communication towers. Span covers natural structures, such as cliffs, arches, or canyons. Earth is any natural or human-made object that is closer to the ground, such as a hill.

BASE jumpers leap off natural high points, such as cliff tops.

EXTREME NEED TO KNOW

BASE jumping is one of the most extreme and high-risk sports. Jumpers must be very skilled, experienced, and careful. They need superb understanding of **aerodynamics** and what to do in an emergency to make sure they jump and land safely.

BASE jumpers head up to high points, then jump!

EXTREME STAR

MULTI-TALENTED

Steph Davis is one of the world's leading climbers and one of the most experienced **free-solo climbers**. And, as if that isn't enough, she also happens to be an awesome BASE jumper and wingsuit flier!

CLIMBING CAREER

Born in 1973, Steph grew up spending more of her time studying and playing music than doing extreme sports. But when she went to college, that all changed. Steph started climbing, fell in love with the sport, and went on to have an amazingly successful career in it.

LOVE TO JUMP

In 2007, Steph began skydiving, and another extreme sport passion was born. But there was a catch—there were no official **drop zones** at that time in Moab, Utah, where Steph lived. So, still determined to enjoy a sky-high sport, she learned to BASE jump instead.

NO FEAR

Steph says she had to face a fear of falling when free-solo climbing, and that skydiving and BASE jumping helped her overcome that fear, and also learn how to deal with other, more general, worries.

THE WORLD'S BEST BASE JUMPS

For air-hungry BASE jumpers, there are some incredible places to leap from. Here are some of the top spots for the world's extreme jumpers.

Perrine Bridge

Where: Idaho, United States

The draw: one of the most famous BASE-jumping sites in the world, it is on every jumper's bucket list

Brento

Where: Italy

The draw: known for its stunning cliffs and **panoramic** views

Lauterbrunnen Valley

Where: Switzerland

The draw: as with wingsuit flying, this is one of the most popular places in the world to BASE jump. Its beautiful cliffs and many different jump sites, including the famous Eiger Mountain, draw in jumpers

Angel Falls

Where: Venezuela

The draw: jumping from the cliffs near the world's tallest waterfall, people can enjoy the amazing surrounding scenery as they freefall

KL Tower

Where: Kuala Lumpur, Malaysia

The draw: an annual event sees BASE jumpers from all around the world leaping from this world-famous 1,381-feet (421 m) tower

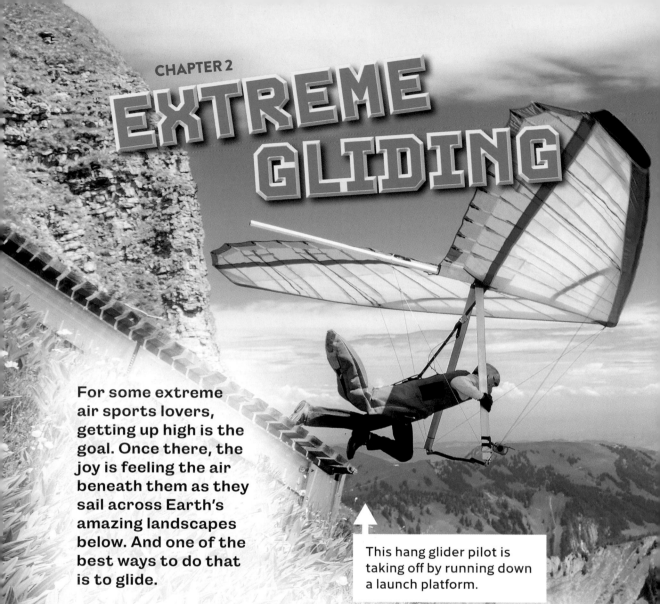

CHAPTER 2

EXTREME GLIDING

For some extreme air sports lovers, getting up high is the goal. Once there, the joy is feeling the air beneath them as they sail across Earth's amazing landscapes below. And one of the best ways to do that is to glide.

This hang glider pilot is taking off by running down a launch platform.

AMAZING TO WATCH, TOUGH TO DO

Gliding sports often use unpowered aircraft, relying only on the natural **forces** of lift and **airflow** to keep the thrill-seeking participants in the air. Others use **motorized** aircraft. To anyone watching from the ground, they all seem to glide with ease. But doing these extreme sports requires a lot of training—and a lot of nerve.

HANG AND GLIDE

Hang gliding is an incredibly popular air sport in which people use a lightweight, unpowered aircraft known as a hang glider, to fly through the sky. The pilot hangs beneath a fabric wing and controls the aircraft by shifting their body weight.

LAUNCH AND LIFT

People can launch gliders by running with them down a slope or launch platform until they lift off. They can also tow the gliders into the air using an aircraft. Once **airborne**, the glider is released. Hang glider pilots use **air currents**, **thermals**, and **ridge lift** to keep them in the air.

ULTIMATE CONTROL

Pilots use a control bar connected to the hang glider's frame to adjust the movement of the aircraft. By pushing or pulling on the control bar, they can change the angle of travel, control the speed, and make turns. When it's time to land, they slowly reduce the hang glider's height and speed. They try to land in a landing zone or an open area with enough space for a safe touchdown.

EXTREME HISTORY

The first known hang glider flight took place in Spain, in CE 875. An inventor named Abbas ibn Firnas made a type of glider from feathers and wood. He launched it and stayed in the air for a short while but his landing was not very smooth. Abbas is said to have come away with a few injuries.

A hang glider has a **rigid** frame, covered with a fabric wing. The wing is often called a sail or wing sail.

"HANG GLIDING—IT'S WHERE YOUR DREAMS CAN FLY AND THE SKY IS YOUR PLAYGROUND."

FREE FLYING

Paragliding is another way for extreme sports lovers to glide through the air. Paragliders sometimes describe their sport as freeflying because they soar through the skies using only a fabric wing to catch the natural air currents and **updrafts**. With the right conditions, paragliders can fly for hours and travel across miles of incredible landscape.

EXTREME GEAR

A paraglider is a lightweight, flexible fabric wing, with a harness attached to it. The pilot is **suspended** beneath the wing in the harness, and uses the brake lines attached to the wing's edge to control the flight.

SPRINT AND SOAR

To launch a paraglider, the pilot runs down a hill or mountain slope while holding the lines so that the wing inflates with air above them. Pilots can also take off from a flat surface by running into the wind. As the air flows over and under the wing, the higher **air pressure** under the wing creates upward lift and launches the paraglider into the air.

EXTREME HISTORY

In the 1960s, the military needed a shortcut when training parachutists in how to land. Instead of putting them on an airplane, then dropping them from the sky, they came up with a simpler and easier way of getting them into the air—with a truck and towrope! Soon, the parachutists decided this was good fun, and started to experiment with catching air currents to float for longer. And so, paragliding was born!

"IF YOU DON'T JUMP, YOU'LL NEVER LEARN TO FLY!"

Some paragliders push the limits of what is possible with incredible stunts in the air.

A lot of panels inflate in the wing of a paraglider to help lift it into the air.

CATCH THE CURRENT

Once in the air, paragliders use the wing to create more lift. By pulling on the lines attached to the back section of the wing, known as the trailing edge, the pilot can control the direction, speed, and **altitude** of the flight. Catching an upward flow of air helps gain height. Skilled paragliders can soar, turn, and stay in the air for an amazingly long time.

TOUCH DOWN

Paragliders land by very slowly traveling toward the ground. They prepare for landing by making turns to lose altitude, or height, while lining themselves up with the landing area. Finally, they touch down on their feet.

SOARING HIGH

Elite paragliders chase **thermal columns** to carry them to dizzying heights before soaring across the landscape in search of their next free ride. Some extreme paragliders even jump off mountains, to catch the upward waves of air at the edge of a ridge for the ultimate ride along a mountain range.

RIDGE SOARING

When wind hits the side of a mountain, it moves upward and forms a band of lift that can last for miles along the slope. In ridge soaring, paragliders catch the currents here for an adrenaline-pumping ride with incredible views.

It takes skill and perfect wind conditions to ridge soar safely.

Climbing a thermal column by turning circles around its core, or center, is called coring.

CURRENT CATCHING

Only the most extreme paragliders risk catching the **turbulent** currents on the other side, or lee side, of the mountain. These air currents can rise way above the mountain peak.

Paragliders brave enough to do this can reach extreme heights of 35,000 feet (10,668 m), or more! At these heights, oxygen levels are low and the winds can be super strong and extremely dangerous. You need a cool head, a plentiful supply of oxygen, and some serious flying skills to glide here!

> "THE SKY IS NOT THE LIMIT. IT'S JUST THE BEGINNING."

EXTREME STAR

PARAGLIDING LEGEND

With multiple world records, four World Championship titles, and two European titles to her name, Seiko Fukuoka from Japan, is a legend in the paragliding world. But, surprisingly, she was not always a fan of the sport.

NOT A FIRST-TIME FAN

When Seiko's father encouraged her to try paragliding for the first time, she wasn't happy—she didn't like the idea of walking up a mountain with a big backpack. Luckily, her father convinced her to give it a try. It wasn't until Seiko saw a video on **acro paragliding** that she became really interested in the extreme sport. Then, in 2003, she moved to Spain to practice acro flying with the **Safety Acro Team**.

CHAMPION TRAINER

In 2009, Seiko took up competitive cross-country paragliding. In this type of paragliding, pilots fly long distances following a particular course. She went on to become one of the best cross-country paragliding pilots in the world. Alongside her own competitions, Seiko now trains other pilots for competitions. Her talent for her sport and dedication to it is an inspiration to others.

THE WORLD'S ULTIMATE GLIDE ZONES

There are some incredible paragliding spots around the world where the panoramic views and thermals make for amazing gliding. These are some of the best.

Interlaken

Where: Switzerland

The draw: with snow-capped peaks and crystal-clear lakes, the thermals and winds here are ideal for both beginners and expert paragliders

Ölüdeniz

Where: Turkey

The draw: sandy beaches, turquoise waters, lush green hills, and the beautiful Blue Lagoon

Chamonix

Where: France

The draw: breathtaking views and challenging flying conditions—expert skills and knowledge are needed here

Rio de Janeiro

Where: Brazil

The draw: lush forests, beautiful beaches, and views of Copacabana Beach, Sugarloaf Mountain, and the Christ the Redeemer statue

Pokhara

Where: Nepal

The draw: great for cross-country flights, endless soaring, and breathtaking views of the Himalaya Mountains

Kamshet

Where: India

The draw: this beautiful, lake-filled area has ideal flying conditions, with gentle winds and thermals

Queenstown

Where: New Zealand

The draw: panoramic views of the Southern Alps, Lake Wakatipu, and the surrounding dramatic landscapes

Cape Town

Where: South Africa

The draw: stunning views of the city, the Atlantic Ocean coastline, and the incredible Table Mountain National Park

City, mountain, or grassy slopes are all playgrounds for speedflier pilots!

"SPEEDFLYING IS TO PARAGLIDING WHAT BASE JUMPING IS TO SKYDIVING."

MADE FOR SPEED

Speedflier pilots use a wing known as a speed wing or mini-wing. It is designed for high speeds, tighter turns, and quick maneuvers. The wing is made from lightweight materials and has a longer, narrower shape than a traditional paraglider. Unlike **speedriders**, speedfliers do not use skis. They launch and land on foot.

FLYING HIGH

Fans of speedflying head for high-up places such as mountain slopes, where they can take a running jump to launch the speed wing. They can be seen on a lot of different mountain areas, including grassy hills and rocky cliffs. Some fans of the sport even take it to towns and cities.

WINGING IT

Speedflying is all about high speeds and fast drops. Elite pilots carve turns and hug the **contours** of a mountain while descending a slope unbelievably quickly. Watch a highly skilled speedflier pilot and you'll see stunning maneuvers performed at spectacular speeds.

SNOW, PLUS WINGS!

For other thrill-seekers, speedriding is an exciting mix of snowboarding or skiing and paragliding. Pilots fly small, high-performance paragliders close to the ground, often traveling down steep slopes at spectacular speeds. This is an extreme sport that combines freedom in the air with an intense adrenaline rush.

EXTREME HISTORY

Speedriding was born from experiments by extreme sportspeople. They decided to mix skiing with paragliding, and speedriding was the result!

One major player in the early days of the sport was François Bon, a French paragliding instructor and test pilot. In the late 1990s, he saw the need for smaller, easier-to-fly paragliders that could travel closer to the ground and that could be coupled with skis.

Then, in the 2000s, another French paraglider and skier named Valentin Delluc released a video that showed him making breathtaking mountain descents wearing skis and a paragliding wing. This caught the attention of the extreme sports community—and speedriding quickly took off.

FAST, FURIOUS, AND HIGH-RISK

Speedflying and speedriding usually take place in mountainous areas, so fans of these extreme sports must have a good understanding of weather conditions, wind patterns, and the dangers of mountain **terrain**.

Speedriding combines the excitement of skiing with the exhilaration of paragliding.

Paramotors can even be launched in the desert.

MIXING IT UP

As with all extreme sports, people often push the sports to the limits. And for some paragliders, adding a motor to the mix was a way to go faster, higher, and for longer.

KIT FOR CLIMBING

Paramotoring is paragliding but with the addition of a small motor called a paramotor. This piece of machinery allows pilots to take off from flat ground and have powered flights. That means they can travel farther and for longer than they can with a paraglider or speedflier.

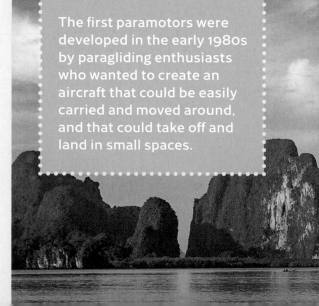

EXTREME HISTORY

The first paramotors were developed in the early 1980s by paragliding enthusiasts who wanted to create an aircraft that could be easily carried and moved around, and that could take off and land in small spaces.

POWERED UP

A paramotor has a wing similar to those used in paragliding, a harness that suspends the pilot beneath the wing, and a fuel tank. It also has a **propeller** and a small engine, which sits on a frame and is attached to the pilot's back.

TAKE-OFF TIME

The pilot launches the paramotor by starting the engine, raising the wing overhead, and running forward. That creates enough speed for the wing to inflate and gain lift. The added **thrust** from the propeller allows the pilot to take off from flat ground. That means they can launch from any large, open area such as a field, beach, or meadow.

FLIGHT CONTROL

Once airborne, the pilot can control the direction, height, and speed of the flight. They do so by adjusting the **throttle** on the engine and by shifting their weight. They also use brakes to control their speed.

FARTHER, FASTER, AND LONGER

Paramotor pilots can stay airborne for several hours at a time, and can reach speeds of around 25 to 45 miles per hour (40 to 72 kph), depending on the wind and other weather conditions.

Paramotors give pilots the chance to travel farther for longer over spectacular landscapes.

GLIDING HIGH

For some extreme air sports fans, staying in the sky for as long as possible is the ultimate goal—and a glider helps them do just that, but with no engine needed! This unpowered aircraft uses just air currents to stay in the sky. Glider pilots seek out updrafts, thermal columns, and ridge lifts to stay airborne all day, often covering huge distances.

BUILT TO SOAR

Gliders are built with lightweight materials to reduce weight, which helps them stay airborne for longer. This allows glider pilots to cover long distances with minimal loss of height. Long, narrow wings reduce drag and increase the gliders' soaring capabilities.

Gliders can be towed by another powered airplane until they are fully airborne.

"GLIDING IS HAPPINESS!"

Gliding above amazing landscapes is one of the top reasons why people take up this sport.

Gliders soar in the air—they are amazing to watch and even more amazing to fly.

WAYS TO LAUNCH

Gliders are launched in two ways, by aerotowing or winch launching. In aerotowing, a powered aircraft tows the glider into the air using a **towline**. In winch launching, a ground-based **winch** quickly reels in a cable attached to the glider, which **propels** it into the air.

GLIDE CONTROL

One or, sometimes, two glider pilots sit in the cockpit. The pilot controls the glider with a control stick or control wheel for pitch control, which means pointing the glider nose up or down. They also use the controls to roll the glider over. The rudder pedals are for yaw control, which means turning left or right.

EXTREME HISTORY

Gliding began in ancient times, with several early inventors jumping from towers with self-made wings in an attempt to glide. In the nineteenth century, George Cayley in England and Otto Lilienthal in Germany came up with the first modern gliders.

Both George and Otto made successful glider flights and devoted themselves to understanding their sport. Otto even became known as the "Glider King," because he spent so much of his life studying flight. Both men paved the way for modern gliders and the extreme sport that gliding has become today.

FLYING HIGHS

Gliding is all about incredible heights, long gliding distances, and breathtaking panoramic views. These are some of the world's most awesome gliding spots.

Mifflin County

Where: Pennsylvania, United States

The draw: ridge soaring and **dynamic soaring** along the spectacular Appalachian Mountains

Minden

Where: Nevada, United States

The draw: strong thermals, long gliding distances, and the incredible Sierra Nevada mountain range

Omarama

Where: New Zealand

The draw: the area is perfect for **wave soaring**, allowing gliders to reach incredible altitudes and fly long distances

Bitterwasser

Where: Kalahari Desert, Namibia

The draw: outstanding thermals and ideal conditions for long-distance gliding making it a favorite spot for record attempts

Oerlinghausen

Where: Germany

The draw: thermal and ridge soaring over the beautiful Teutoburg Forest make this a very popular gliding zone

Lasham

Where: England

The draw: dynamic conditions allow for some exciting ridge soaring and thermal flying over rolling hills

Benalla

Where: Australia

The draw: great weather conditions, reliable thermals, and wide open airspace over awesome countryside

CHAPTER 3

JUMP AND SWING!

How do you combine height, speed, and Earth's amazing landforms and structures? With a rope, a jump, and a hair-raising freefall. Sounds scary? It is, but if you love extreme air sports, the scare is all part of the sport. Welcome to the world of bungee jumping and canyon swinging!

DEATH-DEFYING DROPS

Many people claim that bungee jumping gives an adrenaline rush like nothing else. Jumpers plunge from a great height, while attached to a stretchy cord fitted to their harness, for an adrenaline-pumping freefall before bouncing back up.

EXTREME HISTORY

Bungee jumping has its roots in a land-diving practice called Nangol. It was first practiced by women on Pentecost Island in the Pacific Ocean. These women tied vines around their ankles and jumped from tall wooden towers but the men didn't like seeing their wives in that position, and took over the tradition. The jumps took place for centuries and are still practiced on the island today.

Jumpers say they love the feeling of freedom as they plunge through the air.

TAKING THE PLUNGE

People who are brave enough to take the plunge lean forward from the jumping platform and look straight ahead, with their arms outstretched. Then it's time to dig deep, take a deep breath, and take that leap for the ultimate adrenaline rush.

HEAD FOR HEIGHTS

From purpose-built platforms, bridges, and dams in stunning canyons and valleys to cranes and soaring skyscrapers in panoramic cityscapes, extreme bungee jumpers are always seeking dizzying new heights for the most heart thumping drops.

EXTREME STAR

BUNGEE MASTER

A.J. Hackett is a true **trailblazer** in the world of bungee jumping. Born Alan John Hackett in 1958 in New Zealand, Alan was inspired by the land-diving rituals in the South Pacific and began experimenting with bungee-jumping techniques and equipment.

JUMPING TO FAME

Alan shot to fame in 1987 when he launched himself off the world-famous Eiffel Tower in Paris, France. His incredible bungee jump caught the world's attention and sparked a global bungee-jumping craze.

In 1988, Alan co-founded the world's first **commercial** bungee jumping site—the "Kawarau Bridge Bungy" in Queenstown, New Zealand—with Henry van Asch. Alan went on to set up jumping sites around the world.

A.J. HACKETT LIVED BY HIS MOTTO OF LIVING MORE AND FEARING LESS!

35

GETTING WIRED

Zip lining is another heart-pumping sport for people who want to get up high and race through the air. Zip liners zoom across amazing landscapes ranging from forests and canyons to mountains and **urban** settings. For anyone who loves height and speed, zip lining is the go-to extreme sport.

CROSSING THE LINE

There is a lot of tech behind zip lining. Zip liners are harnessed and suspended from a pulley system, which attaches to a cable that reaches between two platforms. The zip liner soars over landscapes or cityscapes at high speed as the pulley moves along the cable. Zip line courses can have a single line or multiple lines. Some zip lines twist and turn at high speed for an ultimate rush. Others cross wide-open landscapes for an awe-inspiring bird's-eye view.

Zip lining can be an amazing way to have fun, as long as you have a head for heights!

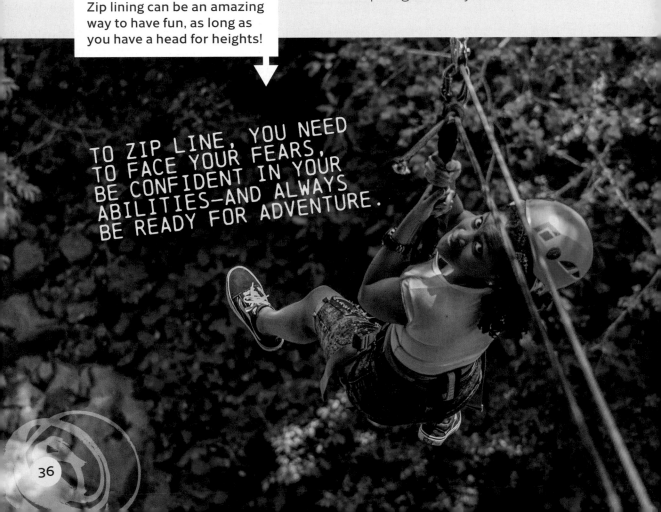

TO ZIP LINE, YOU NEED TO FACE YOUR FEARS, BE CONFIDENT IN YOUR ABILITIES—AND ALWAYS BE READY FOR ADVENTURE.

For safety, most highliners use a back-up leash attached to the line. Highlining without any safety equipment is known as free-solo highlining.

WALKING THE WIRE

Another extreme sport only for those with a cool head for heights is highlining. This sport involves balancing and walking across a narrow line suspended at extreme heights. The line is fixed at two points either side of huge drops between cliffs, rock formations, or buildings. The more dramatic and awe-inspiring the location, the better.

NARROW FOCUS

Highlining demands amazing balance and intense levels of concentration, because the line can be just a few inches wide. Highliners use their **core strength** and focus to maintain stability and control.

EXTREME NEED TO KNOW

Extreme sports come with risks, and highlining is no exception. The sport demands a high level of skill and experience. Extreme sports lovers must first master slacklining, which is walking a slacker line suspended at a low height. They gradually raise the line and become used to walking it at greater heights. Safety gear, including a climbing harness, back-up leash, and helmet must be used at all times.

THE BEST OF THE BUNGEES

What makes a great bungee jump zone? Think awe-inspiring geographical features and famous structures with extreme drops and awesome views. For people brave enough to bungee jump, here are Earth's top places.

Kawarau Bridge

Where: New Zealand

The draw: the world's first commercial bungee jumping site—thrilling jumps from the historic bridge over the Kawarau River make this bungee hot-spot a must

Verzasca Dam

Where: Switzerland

The draw: a 721-feet (220 m) leap made famous by James Bond in the 1995 movie *GoldenEye*

Victoria Falls Bridge

Where: Zimbabwe

The draw: an adrenaline-pumping 364-feet (111 m) drop into the Zambezi River gorge

Macau Tower

Where: China

The draw: people leap from a height of 764 feet (233 m) and freefall toward the bustling cityscape of Macau below

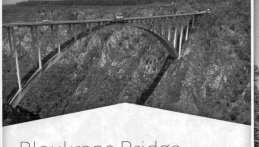

Bloukrans Bridge

Where: South Africa

The draw: a 708-feet (216 m) adrenaline rush above the Bloukrans River

Nevis Highwire Bungy

Where: New Zealand

The draw: an infamous 439-feet (134 m) freefall from a suspended cable car platform in a rugged canyon setting

AJ Hackett Sentosa

Where: Singapore

The draw: a thrilling urban bungee jumping experience, with panoramic views of the city skyline

The Last Resort

Where: Nepal

The draw: a thrilling leap from a 524-feet (160 m) suspension bridge over the roaring Bhote Koshi River

CANYON SWINGING

For some jumpers, the downward drop is the draw but for others, the thrill is in the swing. Canyon swingers take bungee jumping to a whole new level. Canyon swinging combines an adrenaline-pumping bungee jump with the thrill of swinging through awe-inspiring canyons, gorges, and other amazing natural landscapes.

OVER THE EDGE

In canyon swinging, a long, stretchy cord is secured at one end to an anchor point at the edge of a canyon. The other end is attached to the jumper via a harness system. The jumper then either leaps off the cliff—or is pushed off or dropped. Some extreme jumpers are even pushed backward off a chair.

The ropes of the Shotover Canyon Swing near Queenstown, New Zealand, can be seen in this picture.

"IF YOU CAN CANYON SWING, YOU CAN DO JUST ABOUT ANYTHING!"

Taking the plunge takes nerves of steel!

FREEFALL AND SWING

Next comes the rush of the freefall as the jumper plunges down into the canyon. Then, at the end of the drop, the rope's length and **tension** swings the jumper like a pendulum through the canyon and back again.

THE KUSHMA SWING

With a starting point of 748 feet (228 m) above the ground, the Kushma Swing is the highest canyon swing in the world. It is located in Kushma, Nepal. There, adrenaline seekers can either bungee jump or canyon swing from the Kushma Bridge—leaping into the enormous drop below.

TAKING THE PLUNGE

Leaping from the same platform as Kushma bungee jumpers, canyon swingers take less of a vertical plunge and more of a horizontal dive. This allows for a longer freefall of around 8.5 seconds.

INCREDIBLE TO SEE

The Kushma Bridge is itself an incredible sight to behold. It is the longest pedestrian suspension bridge on Earth and it spans the deepest gorge in the world—the Kali Gandaki Gorge. Canyon swing there and you are guaranteed awe-inspiring scenery and a truly amazing experience.

HEART-STOPPING SWINGS

These are some of the incredible canyon-swinging spots around the world, where the views and jumps combine for the ultimate swings.

Monteverde Cloud Forest

Where: Costa Rica

The draw: lush **rain forest** canyons and amazing waterfalls are great to see, but from a 470-foot (143 m) high "tarzan" swing, they look even better!

Grindelwald

Where: Switzerland

The draw: a heart-pumping swing through a narrow gorge, from a 295-foot (90 m) high platform

Minjin Jungle Swing

Where: Australia

The draw: tropical rain forest canyons with lush greenery and the sound of wildlife

Royal Gorge Bridge

Where: Colorado, United States

The draw: swinging out at 50 mph (80 kph), 1,200 feet (366 m) above the deep, red canyon of the Arkansas River

The Last Resort

Where: Nepal

The draw: one of the world's biggest canyon swings, with incredible scenery

Shotover Canyon Swing

Where: New Zealand

The draw: the thrill of swinging through the incredible Shotover River canyon (see page 40)

acro paragliding creating acrobatic movements such as loops and turns while paragliding

adrenaline a hormone, or chemical messenger in the body, that creates a sense of excitement and a surge of energy

aerial acrobatics impressive moves such as somersaults that are done in the air

aerodynamics the study of how objects move through the air

air currents areas of wind created by changes in air pressure or temperature

air pressure the force created by air when it comes into contact with an object

airborne to be fully in the air

airflow the flow of air along an aircraft or vehicle

altitude the height of an object above sea level

athletes people who take part in sports, often competing at a high level

BASE jumper a person who takes part in the extreme sport of BASE jumping. BASE jumping involves parachuting or wingsuit flying from fixed objects, such as buildings, antennas, bridges, or cliffs

bungee jumping leaping from a high place while attached to a fixed object with a long, flexible band

canyon swing leap from a high place above a canyon while attached to a fixed object with a long, flexible band, before swinging like a pendulum

commercial money-making

contours the outlines of a shape, such as a mountain

core strength strength around the abdomen and back

descent a downward journey, usually on a mountain

drag the force exerted on an object that slows it as the object passes through air

drop zones places where skydiving is allowed

dynamic soaring a flying technique used to gain energy by repeatedly crossing the boundary between air masses of different speed

elite the best at something

endure to withstand

exhilarating very exciting, thrilling, and pleasurable

extreme sports high-risk sports that push sportspeople to their limits

fjords long, narrow bodies of inland water with high cliffs on either side

flexible easily bends

flight paths planned flight journeys

forces pushes and pulls

free-solo climbers people who climb without ropes and certain protective equipment

freefall to fall rapidly toward the ground while unattached to any restraining device

gliding staying in and traveling through the air often in unpowered aircraft using only the upward lift of the air

gorges narrow valleys between hills or mountains, usually with steep rocky walls and a stream running through them

gravity the force that pulls objects toward other large objects

grueling extremely demanding and exhausting

highline to walk on a suspended line that is stretched between two anchor points at considerable height

land formations features on Earth's surface such as mountains and valleys

maneuvers moves around something

motorized equipped with a motor

newbie a person who is a beginner or new to something

panoramic a wide, sweeping view

pendulum an object that is suspended from a fixed point and that swings back and forth because of gravity

plummets falls very quickly

propeller a piece of machinery that spins quickly in air or water to move a vehicle forward

propels pushes forward

rain forest a forest that receives a lot of rainfall

ridge lift rising air along the side of a slope

rigid very firm

Safety Acro Team a team of paragliders who perform acrobatic tricks

scale the act of climbing a vertical or steep surface

skydiving jumping from an airplane wearing a parachute and then traveling to the ground

sound barrier the sudden increase in resistance that the air gives an aircraft nearing the speed of sound

speedriders athletes who participate in speedriding, which is a type of paragliding that uses a ski to descend, or come down, a mountain

spread-eagle position a position in which the arms and legs are held outward, like a flying bird

stratosphere the second layer of Earth's atmosphere as you go upward

surface area the area of a person or object over which water or air can pass

suspended held in the air

tension tightness and rigidity

terrain the physical characteristics of a particular area of land. Terrain can range from flat and open to rugged and mountainous

thermal columns areas of rising air that carry heat upward

thermals rising bodies of warm air

throttle a device that helps control the speed of a vehicle

thrust a powerful forward movement

towline a rope or chain used to tow a person or vehicle

trailblazer the first person to do something that many other people then follow

trunk the main part of the body that contains the chest, abdomen, pelvis, and back

turbulent describes air that is moving unsteadily or very strongly

updrafts upward movements of air

urban areas with a high number of people and buildings, such as towns and cities

wave soaring when a glider flies along vertical waves of wind that form on the lee side of mountain ranges (the side protected from fiercer winds)

winch a spool that turns around and that can tighten or loosen a cable

FIND OUT MORE

BOOKS

DISCOVER MORE ABOUT EXTREME SPORTS WITH THESE GREAT READS.

Bailey, Diane. *Skydiving* (Intense Sports). Rourke Educational Media, 2015.

Eason, Sarah. *Dig Deep! Extreme Land Sports* (Ultimate Sports). Cheriton Children's Books, 2024.

Eason, Sarah. *Freeze Your Fear! Extreme Snow and Ice Sports* (Ultimate Sports). Cheriton Children's Books, 2024.

Eason, Sarah. *Take a Deep Breath! Extreme Water Sports* (Ultimate Sports). Cheriton Children's Books, 2024.

Mooney, Carla. *Skydiving* (Sports to the Extreme). Rosen Publishing, 2015.

Uhl, Xina M. *Extreme Aerial Silks* (Sports to the Extreme). Rosen Publishing, 2020.

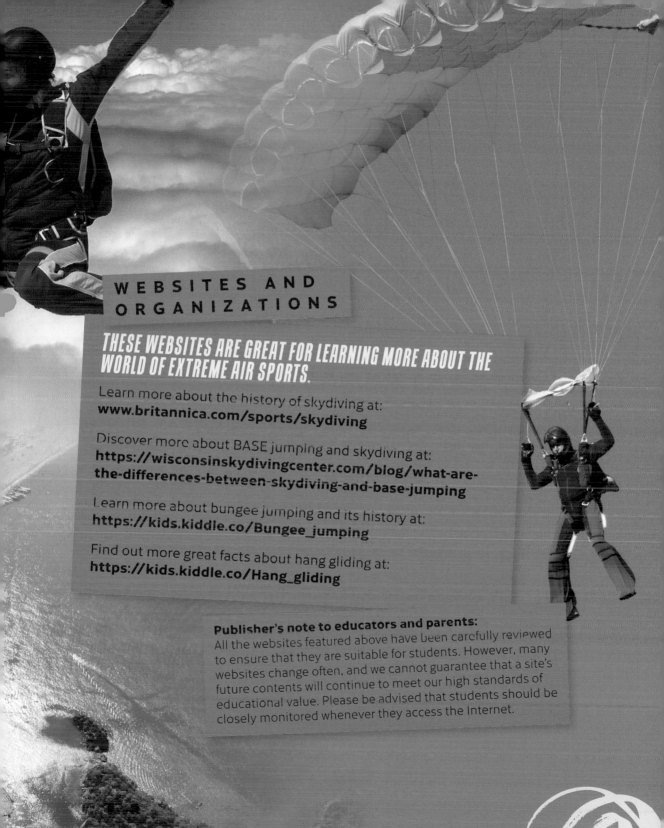

WEBSITES AND ORGANIZATIONS

THESE WEBSITES ARE GREAT FOR LEARNING MORE ABOUT THE WORLD OF EXTREME AIR SPORTS.

Learn more about the history of skydiving at:
www.britannica.com/sports/skydiving

Discover more about BASE jumping and skydiving at:
https://wisconsinskydivingcenter.com/blog/what-are-the-differences-between-skydiving-and-base-jumping

Learn more about bungee jumping and its history at:
https://kids.kiddle.co/Bungee_jumping

Find out more great facts about hang gliding at:
https://kids.kiddle.co/Hang_gliding

Publisher's note to educators and parents:
All the websites featured above have been carefully reviewed to ensure that they are suitable for students. However, many websites change often, and we cannot guarantee that a site's future contents will continue to meet our high standards of educational value. Please be advised that students should be closely monitored whenever they access the Internet.

INDEX

ABOUT THE AUTHOR

Sarah Eason is an experienced children's book author who has written many books about sport and sport science. She would love to visit some of the amazing places researched while writing this book, and (maybe!) try out some extreme sports there.